IMAGES
of America

ROSCOE

On the Cover: During the 1907–1908 school year, Roscoe Grade School students gather on the wooden porch in front of the school. The four-room, redbrick building was erected in 1855, a block north of the Methodist church on Main Street. Before it was built, school was housed in many other locations, with the first classes being held in the spring of 1837 at Reynolds's blacksmith shop, followed by a small, wooden-frame building on Elevator Road, and then the Methodist Episcopal church basement. The first day of classes in the new brick building began with a procession of students led by the principal, D.C. Smith, from the church up the hill to the new classrooms. This building served Roscoe's students until 1948, when Kinnikinnick School was built. (Courtesy of Dorothy Hunter.)

IMAGES
of America

ROSCOE

Dorothy Hunter with Doris Hunter Tropp

ARCADIA
PUBLISHING

Published by Arcadia Publishing
Charleston, South Carolina

Library of Congress Control Number: 2013931010

For all general information, please contact Arcadia Publishing:
Telephone 843-853-2070
Fax 843-853-0044
E-mail sales@arcadiapublishing.com
For customer service and orders:
Toll-Free 1-888-313-2665

Visit us on the Internet at www.arcadiapublishing.com

This book is dedicated to all those who love Roscoe and its
history and who helped make this book possible, including
the pioneers who carved our village out of the prairie.

CONTENTS

ACKNOWLEDGMENTS

The following poem expresses the sentiments of many Roscoe residents:

Roscoe—My Village of Memories
by Verna McDonald Bittrick

So full of pleasure, small town living
Loving people, warm and giving
Some memories I hold and keep
Like quiet walks along the creek
Wilcox Woods with Dutchman's breeches
The southern Ledges rocky reaches
The baseball games on our back lot
And playing in the blacksmith shop
The railroad culvert swimming hole
My brothers with their fishing pole
The winter nights so calm and still.
While sledding up at Ponsor's hill
Ice skating parties at the creek,
Then back to Fry's to warm our cheeks
Town Hall dances on Saturday night,
With children too, a sheer delight
The festival pageant in the fall
The annual symphony at the hall
Hobart's berries, oh so sweet
The popcorn stand out by the street

Mr. Bender's melon patch
Our oriole nest with eggs to hatch
The Ransom mansion rife with charm
And shooting pool in Stultz's barn
And was there ever such a place,
As Mr. Ransom's candy case
The playhouse up at Deatie's home,
With barns and fields in which to roam
My twin and me and our 'swimming pool'
And our paper routes right after school
Out in the orchard climbing trees
Roller skates and banged up knees
The heated bricks to warm our bed
The bedtime stories mother read
Under the covers so Mom wouldn't know,
The "I Love A Mystery" show
On and on, so much to tell,
And if I had a wishing well,
I'd make a wish and turn back time,
And give each child a youth like mine.

Unless otherwise noted, all images appear courtesy of the author.

INTRODUCTION

Before 1835, the area along the Rock River in the northeast corner of Winnebago County was inhabited by Potawatomi and Winnebago tribes who used the vast prairie land as a common hunting ground. They could be seen going in all directions to and from Stephen Mack's trading post, then located on the north bank of the Rock River below the mouth of the dry run, in an area called Bird's Grove.

Bird's Grove later became part of Hononegah Forest Preserve, which was named, like many things in the area, after Stephen Mack's Native American wife, Princess Ho-No-Ne-Gah. The phonetic spelling of her name has been Anglicized in pronunciation and the hyphens eliminated—except in the formal name of the area high school and use on items such as diplomas and crests, where the hyphenated version is seen side-by-side with the Anglicized spelling, Hononegah.

The remains of cabins belonging to earlier Indian traders could still be seen. Maple trees showed evidence that they had been tapped by the Indians for maple sugar many years earlier. Wagon tracks made in June 1832 by Gen. Henry Atkinson as he followed Black Hawk through the middle of the future town were still visible. An old Indian trail called the Round Prairie Road led from Rockton through what would be Roscoe and Caledonia to the camp of Chief Big Thunder on the banks of the Kishwaukee River at Belvidere. Portions of that old trail became Hononegah Road and Elevator Road.

Robert J. Cross, Roscoe's first settler, and Colonel von Hovenburg arrived from Coldwater, Michigan, on August 3, 1835, with an Indian guide. The colonel returned to Michigan, but Cross bought a claim from a man named Lavec, an employee of Stephen Mack, the fur trader who had settled in the Rockton area in 1829. Cross spent about 10 days putting up hay and exploring, going down the river toward Rockford. When he returned in October, he brought along farming tools and a man named Robert Logan.

In September 1835, Elijah H. Brown, James B. Lee, and William Mead came from LaPorte County, Indiana. Brown built the first cabin in the township, a little above the north branch of Kinnikinnick Creek, and Lee built the second house near the road to Beloit. William Mead became the first settler south of the Roscoe area, at Harlem.

Cross built a cabin on his claim along the river, which came to be known as Cross Grove and was a popular spot for picnicking and gathering walnuts. It is now part of the Edgemere Terrace area. Between 1841 and 1843, Cross built a brick home that still stands at 4562 Hononegah Road.

Cross, Lee, Brown, and Logan were the only settlers in the area that first winter. Cross owned the only horse team and was kept busy all winter hauling flour and other supplies back from Chicago. When ready to leave, he would pack $10-15 worth of oats on top of his load to feed the horses along the way.

John Lovesee and Ferris Thayer arrived November 17, 1835, with Cross, who had been in Chicago. They brought along a small grindstone—the first one north of Rockford—which they carried about a fourth of the way on their backs with a stick through the hole as they traveled through ankle- to knee-deep water and often heavy snow. With no roads or bridges, the trip from

Chicago took seven days. Today, the same trip can be made in about an hour. Lovesee spent the winter with Stephen Mack and returned to Roscoe in 1836. His brother William Lovesee also arrived in 1836 after walking barefoot all the way from Chicago, carrying his shoes most of the way to keep from wearing them out. He later helped Caleb Blodgett build the first house in Beloit, Wisconsin.

Ruben Bennett came in the late summer of 1836, and in September, Russell Brayton, Simon Secoy, and Cory Taft arrived. Benjamin Richardson II of Gloversville, New York, had recently moved his family to Michigan when he heard glowing reports of the Rock River country in Illinois from those who had followed Black Hawk with General Atkinson. Richardson traveled west to investigate and, liking what he found, immediately returned to Michigan for his wife and two children, the youngest of whom was just six months old when they left New York. He purchased an oxteam and set out for Illinois. In Ohio, they met the Smith Jenks family heading west, and the two families traveled together as far as Chicago before going their separate ways.

On arriving at the top of a hill overlooking the prairie in Roscoe, the Richardsons saw another wagon coming from the opposite side. They were amazed to discover their friends, the Smith Jenks family, arriving at the same time in the same place after having split earlier. The two families arrived at sunset on October 17, 1836, and wintered together near the bank of the South Kinnikinnick Creek.

Another 1836 arrival was Andrew Reynolds of Indiana, who bought Lee's claim and was the first blacksmith in the area. His shop was said to have been on the south bank of North Kinnikinnick Creek near the road to Beloit.

Walter Warner also came in 1836 and homesteaded land south of Roscoe on what is now Swanson Road. In the fall, he returned to Lima, New York, and the following spring he sent his family with that of his brother-in-law Norris Wilcox by canal to Buffalo, where they then embarked on a three-week sailing trip across the Great Lakes to Chicago. The men drove a team with their belongings overland from New York to Illinois, where they joined their families and arrived in Roscoe August 8, 1837.

Amos Tuttle moved his family to Roscoe in 1837, as did Andrew James Lovejoy and Thomas Baldwin.

Rev. Dudley Greeley, a Methodist preacher, and his family came in spring 1837. Rev. Albert Tuttle, a local Methodist preacher, was also an early settler.

In 1838, Dr. Solomon Jenks, Roscoe's first physician and the brother of Smith Jenks, came west with his eldest son. He bought up several claims and in July began the trip back to Ohio for his remaining family members. Before the year's end, on Christmas Eve 1838, he started his return trip to Roscoe. He built a log cabin south of Kinnikinnick Creek on the west side of Main Street, later the site of the beautiful Ransom home built in 1869 and destroyed by fire in 1985.

Alvan and Solomon Leland also arrived in 1838. Horatio Leonard's family came in 1839, as did the Patten Atwood family, who had earlier moved from New England to Canada and, after hearing about Illinois, relocated to Roscoe.

From only four settlers during the winter of 1836, the little community grew to over 50 people in the next four years. In 1842, James Thompson arrived and built a woolen factory, gristmill, foundry, and distillery, and in 1855 the railroad was built and Roscoe became a bustling, enterprising community.

Early Roscoe citizens were religious and opposed alcohol consumption and slavery. They were civic minded, neighborly, and hardworking, always ready to pitch in and come together for the betterment of their village. As Quincy Dowd, the Congregational Church minister, said in a 1906 historical address, "those early pioneers were a sober, pious, temperate, thrifty class and they all went to church."

One

THE BIG FUNDRAISER

Rev. Quincy Dowd, Congregational Church pastor, and his wife, Nellie, are pictured in front of the church parsonage across from Roscoe's village park. On May 10, 1910, Dowd led a group of concerned citizens as they sought to better their village by forming the Roscoe Improvement Association. To raise money for future projects, they decided to hold a festival the following September.

The Roscoe Improvement Association

WILL HOLD AN ALL-DAY

Fair and Festival

Saturday, Sept. 17, '10

at ROOSEVELT PARK

A GRAND PARADE OF

Floats and Automobiles, Live Stock and Various Attractive Features at 10:00 o'clock under the direction of Marshall R. R. Allen

Display of Domestic Arts, Curios and Relics, Agricultural Products and Flowers at the Town Hall

Exhibition of Live Stock, Pets and Poultry at the Park

BARBECUE--12:00 o'clock
(PICNIC DINNER)

Speaking and Sports in the Park

CHAIRMEN OF EXHIBITS

Domestic Arts	Mrs. H. B. Curtis
Flowers	Mrs. Will Lovesee
Curios and Relics	Bertha Hutchins
Live Stock	Kay McCurry
Agricultural Products	Ed. Youngs
Pet Stock	Lee Wilcox
Sports	Roy Cummings

Premiums Awarded

President, A. J. LOVEJOY   Secretary, MARY F. FYLER

V. R. LIND, PRINTER   ROCKFORD, ILL.

The first Roscoe Fall Festival was held September 17, 1910, as advertised on this poster. The notices were distributed throughout the village of about 300 people. (Courtesy of Robert Lawhorn.)

The chief drawing card of the first Fall Festival in 1910 was a Kentucky-style barbecue. A deep pit lined with live coals was covered with a large homemade grill and tended throughout the night as a yearling steer and two lambs were roasted. The ladies served hot sandwiches, coffee, doughnuts, and pie. A local newspaper reported 1,000 people from outside the village attended.

To be sure of a good crowd for the first Fall Festival in 1910, a group went on an all-day ride with a noon picnic beside the road to persuade each area school to enter a float in the grand parade. The intermediate department of the Roscoe Grade School, representing Winnebago Indians, entered this group that first year.

The primary department of the Roscoe Grade School entered this float in the first parade in 1910. Mae Schmelt, Nellie Budd, and Fern Blackinton are some of the children in the picture. It was Nellie Dowd's idea to enlist a parade float from each department in Roscoe and one from each country school in the area. She knew that if the children participated, their parents would come.

At the first Fall Festival on September 17, 1910, the Girls Club presented a play at the town hall, located a short distance west of the park. The town hall was used for dances, displays, and other activities during the festival. The large canvas stage curtain, filled with advertisements, rolled down from the top. A portion of the advertisements is visible at the top of the rolled-up curtain in the picture.

SCOE FAIR WAS BIG SUCCESS

t Gathering of Its Kind Held
a t u r day   Under   Favorable
Veather—Big Crowds from Many
ounties Were Present.

oscoe, Sept. 19.—Far exceeding
expectations of the board of man-
rs of the event of Saturday, Sept.
1910, was the greatest in the
ory of Roscoe. Even the weath-
man smiled on the little village
le rain fell in both Rockford and
oit.

s early as 8 o'clock the usually
t village began to take on signs
activity and until long after the
n hour crowds came in autos, in
et cars and in carriages, and Ros-
fair and carnival was success-
y launched. Soon after the ap-
ited hour, martial music heralded
coming of the parade, which was
ed great. Mr. R. R. Allen in his
o as marshal of the day, headed
procession; by his side, Hon. A.
ovejoy, as president of the Ros-
Improvement Association; fol-
ing in line were the floats repre-
ting the different schools of the
township. Roscoe high school represented the different nations; the
intermediate department was finel
gotten up as Winnebago Indians
with the wigwam and warwhoop; the
fairies and elves and flower girl
came from the primary department
and represented much time and in
terest on the part of parent as wel
as pupil. The plantation scene
with the little darkies enjoying thei
watermelon feast, the sunflowe
float, the old woman in the shoe
Maple Lawn, Riverside, Wilcox and
Hobart floats all are worthy of es
pecial mentions, as with the nation
al colors, grains, fruits, fowls, live
stock and domestic animals made the
parade one of extreme interest. Man
amusing features were introduced
From Roescoe's most stylish dress
making emporium came the hobbl
skirt lady, fearfully and wonderful
ly gotten up; an old time convey
ance from the Dr. Ransom collection
of vehicles, with an old white hors
to match, created much amusemen
as it moved along the principa
streets, returning to Roosevelt Park
where for two hours barbecued bee
and mutton, coffee and sandwiche
were of interest. No estimate o
the numbers fed could accurately b
made, but near the thousan
mark.

Published two days after the first Roscoe Fall Festival on September 17, 1910, this newspaper article describes the event as "the greatest in the history of Roscoe." It goes on to say, "even the weather man smiled on the little village while rain fell in both Rockford and Beloit," the two towns north and south of Roscoe. The Roscoe Fall Festival is still in existence and is the oldest and longest-running town festival in the area. (Courtesy of the North Suburban Library.)

For the 1910 festival, Frank Sturtevant dressed as a woman, wearing a fashionable pink-and-green hobble skirt. He walked in the first parade to advertise the sewing skills of Matie (or Mate) Rogers, a local seamstress.

This is the 1913 float from Windy Peak School, located a few miles north of Roscoe near the present Rockton Road and Highway 251 intersection. The students of teacher Laura Holmes portray "farmer boys" and "housekeeping girls." (Courtesy of the North Suburban Library.)

This 1913 view of Main Street looks north from in front of the Masonic block. The man in the foreground, J.B. McEachren, is an auctioneer from Argyle, in town for the festival. (Courtesy of the North Suburban Library.)

A later view of Leland Park shows it being readied for another Fall Festival. The block, originally called Roosevelt Park, had been donated for use as a park by Alvan Leland when the village was platted in 1841. On July 4, 1903, after being closed for improvements, it was reopened with a celebration that included a twilight picnic, speakers, music, and fireworks. At that time, it was renamed Leland Park after its donor.

Floats move along the parade route in 1913. (Courtesy of the North Suburban Library.)

Teacher Gladys Shockley accompanies the 1913 Roscoe Grade School float in this picture. (Courtesy of the North Suburban Library.)

This elaborate and colorful 1914 parade float filled with little Roscoe Primary grade "sunbeams" is on its way to be judged at the festival. (Courtesy of Norman Cummings.)

This 1914 Roscoe Grade School Intermediate Department float honors the Red Cross with students dressed as nurses. The Red Cross was included in several pageants, particularly in 1940 and 1941 during a safety pageant titled *You Bet Your Life*. (Courtesy of Norman Cummings.)

In 1914, the horse-drawn Roscoe High School float moves along the parade route with flags and costumes representing various countries. (Courtesy of Norman Cummings.)

This 1914 parade entry carries students from Burr Oak School, a one-room country school located at the corner of Burr Oak and Crockett Roads, a few miles east of town. (Courtesy of Norman Cummings.)

18

In 1914, a float titled *The Old and the New* featured current and previous ladies' fashions. The models are, from left to right, Mrs. George Sally, unidentified, Myrtle Randall, Mabel Roth, Mrs. George Britton, Lida Paine, Mary Reymour, Susan Whitlock, two unidentified women, and Bertha Richardson.

"Pioneers" and their covered wagons were a part of the 1918 pageant, representing the early settlers and their struggles to exist and carve out a living on the prairie. (Courtesy of the North Suburban Library.)

Native Americans were represented in Roscoe's first Fall Festival Pageant in 1918. Roscoe became famous throughout the area for its colorful and elaborate original historical and topical pageants, performed by casts of 300 or more citizens. Nearly everyone in town became involved in some way. The pageants were narrated scenes set to music. (Courtesy of the North Suburban Library.)

In 1918, Illinois governor Frank Lowden called on communities in the state to help celebrate the Illinois Centennial. This prompted Alice McCurry to write a historical pageant, which was performed at the Roscoe Fall Festival on August 23, 1918, and was repeated in September as a Red Cross benefit. This was the first of many pageants written by McCurry to be presented at the festivals. (Courtesy of the North Suburban Library.)

A Lincoln-Douglas debate was reenacted during the 1918 pageant, with Giles Lovesee portraying Lincoln, Roy Muchmore, Douglas, and Frank Sturtevant acting as the chairman. Uncle Sam was played by Joe Gsell; the Prairie Queen, by Mrs. Ira Henderson; Stephen Mack, by Leon Cummings; and Princess Ho-No-Ne-Gah, by Louise Sturtevant. Mary and Ethel Wilcox sang as Mr. and Mrs. Lee Wilcox portrayed "The Soldiers' Farewell" scene. (Courtesy of the North Suburban Library.)

A line of six school floats stretches out in the 1920 parade, with each one representing a 50-year segment for a total of 300 years of American history. Alice Dodge McCurry assigned 50-year segments from 1620 to 1920 to each participating school. (Courtesy of the North Suburban Library.)

These panoramic photographs show the assembled cast and audience of the 1921 Fall Festival pageant, *Cycle of Time*. The pageant took the audience throughout the months of a year, celebrating the four seasons and each month with performances of music and dance. Homage was paid to Father Time and the important holidays. It also included some unofficial holidays, such as Clean-up

Day, the Dog Days, Tag Day, the longest and shortest days, and, of course, Fall Festival Day. The 1921 pageant was repeated in 1959 at the 50th anniversary of the Fall Festival in a performance that featured relatives of the original actors.

This Modern Woodmen float was entered in the 1921 parade. Participants riding on the float are, from left to right, Neil Lindroth, unidentified, Verne Clothier, James B. Hardy and Glenn Baldwin. Modern Woodmen's goat is also riding along. Many lodges of the time period referred to the initiation of new members as "riding the goat." (Courtesy of the North Suburban Library.)

The 1930 Fall Festival pageant was called *The Quest of Youth*, and this picture shows a segment called "The Gate of Life." (Courtesy of the North Suburban Library.)

In the 1935 pageant, *Out of the Past*, many early settlers were portrayed by their descendants. In this picture, Gladys Sturtevant and her five-year-old daughter, Beryl, portray ancestors who settled in the area in the 1840s. Also pictured are Lenore Warner and her daughter Dorothy, age four, portraying Indians.

The 1937 Fall Festival poster advertising the Constitution-themed pageant on September 12 is done in the Art Deco style and includes a silhouette of a statue of Columbia. This pageant was first performed in 1936. (Courtesy of the North Suburban Library.)

PAGEANT

The
CONSTITUTION
of the
UNITED STATES

Presented by the Roscoe Improvement Association

SAT. SEPT. 12TH
10 A.M.   7:30 P.M.
ROSCOE, ILLINOIS
•
DINNER
BALL GAME
ENTERTAINMENT
DANCING

ROSCOE FALL FESTIVAL

The Constitution of the United States pageant was written by Alice Dodge McCurry and Jennie Richardson. An artist, McCurry also painted the amazingly realistic backdrop. The pageant coincided with the 149th anniversary of the Constitution and was performed by a cast of 400. An estimated crowd of over 2,500 attended the first performance. This photograph shows the unveiling of the Constitution by "Columbia," portrayed by Gladys Sturtevant. In the foreground surrounding the constitution are, from left to right, Barbara Gair, Myrtle Mahler, Louise Hall, Helen Lyford, Pete Goff, Vera Silbaugh, Mary Robertson, Verna Mosher, and Betty Russell, who represent ideals and human rights upheld in the constitution. (Courtesy of Norman Cummings.)

The early festival program booklets were about 20 pages and contained a listing of events, the program for the pageant, a scorecard for the ball game, and advertisements for area businesses.

From approximately the 1950s through the 1980s, a Kiddie Parade was held on Saturday morning during each Fall Festival. Cash prizes or savings bonds were awarded in several categories, including prettiest, funniest, and most original. The short parade down Broad Street was a favorite event, with entries becoming more elaborate each year until the judges declared it was impossible to pick the best. The contest was discontinued and replaced with special children's entertainment with a treat and attendance prize raffle for amusement ride wristbands.

Widow Warner Opens School, Dec. 24, 1838

PROGRAM

CENTENNIAL

26th Annual

FALL FESTIVAL
September 14, 1935
Roscoe, Illinois

In the 1967 Kiddie Parade, this group of sisters won the most original award for portraying "what little girls are made of." Seven-year-old Nola Hunter (left) is "Sugar," five-year-old Doris Hunter (center) is "Spice," and three-year-old Laura Hunter is "Everything Nice."

After Roscoe incorporated in 1965 and the Roscoe Improvement Association disbanded, the Lions Club took over sponsorship of the Fall Festival. At its first festival in 1971, a new Dodge automobile was raffled off as the grand prize, a custom that continued for many years. The Lions Club members shown in the photograph are, from left to right, George Palmer, Verne Peters, Al Lenius, and Lloyd Teed. (Courtesy of the Roscoe Lions Club.)

Two

WATER AND RAILS

In this c. 1926 photograph, Elmer Warner is trying out his climbing skills on the Rock River Bridge to impress his fiancée.

People wait for a ride on an excursion boat at the river. Groups like Modern Woodmen often took short, annual summer outings on paddleboats.

The Modern Woodmen society was quite active in the area and often held outings for its members. Here, the *May Lee*, an excursion steam paddleboat, gives passengers a ride on the Rock River near Roscoe. Excursion boats on the river did not last because the waterway was not deep enough for the larger boats to travel north to Beloit, as was originally intended.

This view of the steel bridge over the Rock River at Roscoe is what a traveler would see just before crossing. The water is in flood stage in this picture.

The steel bridge over the river at Roscoe was built at the end of River Street near the present entrance to Riverside Park. It was narrow, with room for one car at a time, and there was a sharp turn at each end.

This picture from February 9, 1900, shows the Rock River Bridge at high-water mark.

A river ferry crossed the river at the foot of River Street near the place where the bridge was later built. William Hale, the first person to be buried in the town cemetery, drowned near the mouth of the creek on June 27, 1837, while trying to save a boy who had fallen off the ferry.

This view of the Rock River Bridge is looking upstream at the beginning of a bend in the river, which curves in a large loop to the west before turning back east, toward the town. The steel bridge was built around 1855 and was dismantled in 1968 when the new, cement, double-lane bridge was constructed.

On Valentine's Day 1918, both sides along the Kinnikinnick Creek east of the bridge in the center of Roscoe were flooded. In the distance is the footbridge leading to the Thompson mills and house.

The homesite of the Roy Cummings family, directly north of the bridge on the east side of Main Street, had a steep bank and several feet of level land next to the creek, which flooded to more than twice its normal size in February 1918. The home is no longer standing.

Nearly every spring, the Rock River flooded over the road on the west side of the bridge because of the melting ice and snow. People living west of the river were forced to use the river bridge in Rockton to drive to Roscoe.

On June 20, 1937, the rain-weakened Main Street Bridge across Kinnikinnick Creek collapsed as a car was crossing. This picture is looking south from the ruined bridge. The house in the distance still stands south of Roscoe's present-day police station.

This automobile fell into the collapsed Main Street Kinnikinnick Creek Bridge while crossing during a cloudburst. While the new bridge was being built, a wooden footbridge was erected on the west side for children and others going to school, church, stores, and the post office on the north side of town. Until the new bridge was finished, automobiles had to travel many extra miles to the west or east to get from one end of town to the other.

This 1937 view of the collapsed Main Street Bridge from the northwest shows the Ransom home, which was located south of the bridge on the former Jenks property. The home no longer stands.

This east-facing view of the collapsed Main Street Bridge does not show the car trapped within the wreckage. Main Street in Roscoe became part of the Illinois state highway system beginning in 1920. It was upgraded to concrete and designated as Illinois State Highway 51 until the bypass was built two blocks west of Main Street in the 1960s.

On September 16, 1899, James W. Smith shows off the black bass he caught in the Rock River at Cross Grove, an area owned by Robert J. Cross that was a favorite spot for fishing and recreation.

A couple digs for clams on the bank of the river. Besides digging clams for themselves, in the earlier days, locals were hired by a commercial clamming industry to work on the clamming boats and gather clams from the river bottom. Clamshells were much in demand in those days for making buttons.

The eastern section of the steel Keeler Bridge, also known as the "Black Bridge," on River Street is seen here. The bridge, which was built in 1898, is still in existence but is no longer open to vehicular traffic.

Dudley Ward stands near an area along the river that belonged to the Moore family. Known as Camp Frolic, it was a popular spot for picnics.

The Chicago & Galena Railroad (later the Chicago & North Western) came to Roscoe around 1855 after the 1827 discovery of lead in Galena. A group of Chicago men led by Chicago's first mayor, William Ogden, hoped to transport the ore back via a new railroad line. Because of the depression of 1837 and 1838, work on the line was not begun until 1845. The tracks entered the village diagonally across the north edge of Roscoe behind the cemetery before curving east toward Caledonia and Chicago.

This Chicago & North Western train ticket is made of heavy card stock. The first-class ticket from Roscoe to Beloit, Wisconsin, is dated June 25, 1886, and the back is stamped "Aug. 13, 1886." The 100-year-old ticket was discovered in the 1980s in an old desk that once belonged to Bertha Sturtevant, wife of Frank Sturtevant.

The train depot provided a small room for waiting passengers. An old coal- or wood-burning stove, much needed during the winter, is visible at left. Coal and other freight could be unloaded and stored at the site; freight could be loaded and unloaded; and passengers could embark on their travels, no longer restricted to horse and wagon or stagecoach. Freight service continued until the line was abandoned in 1984.

Passengers waited inside the small depot. The land for the elevator and depot was donated in the 1850s by Henderson Coffin, who owned three brickyards on property north of the site. The railroad eventually discontinued its passenger service, and in 1965 the depot was dismantled and moved to Edgerton, Wisconsin, for the park operated by the Rock River Thresheree Association.

The southbound Chicago & North Western train travels past the grain elevator and across Elevator Road in the early 1900s. The depot can be seen on the left, a short distance north of the elevator. In the 1990s, the tracks were removed and the train bed was converted to a recreation path. It became part of the Stone Bridge Trail, which is connected to an intercounty trail system.

The 9:30 a.m. train crosses the 1882 stone, double-arch bridge on its way east to Chicago. This culvert was built after the first embankment and smaller culvert collapsed during a spring flood on June 3, 1858. The flood swept away the wife and eight children of Congregational Church pastor Rev. Horatio Ilsley and destroyed nine buildings, including two homes and the 1840s Thompson factories and mills.

The 9:30 a.m. train crosses the creek over the stone bridge behind the cemetery as an unidentified child and dog wait nearby. Before World War II, six trains a day stopped at Roscoe. The Chicago & North Western Railway Stone Arch Bridge (or the Kinnikinnick Creek Railway Bridge) has been listed in the National Register of Historic Places since 1993, while the surrounding prairie has been preserved with Illinois State Conservation status.

A steam work train was used to carry the gravel and rails needed to build the new extension to the RB&J Company electric interurban train, which ran from 1902 until 1930 down the center of Main Street. For each trip, the train ran on the new track with the needed supplies, extended the line, and returned south for additional material, repeating the process.

The steam work train can be seen from the doorway of Lorenzo Fyler's store on Main Street, as it brings rails, gravel and ties for the new interurban, which began service in 1902. The RB&J Company interurban was named to incorporate the initials of the three major cities it served—Rockford, Beloit, and Janesville. The track passed through lesser towns as well, including Roscoe.

Harold McRoberts waits for the approaching interurban car outside the Masonic block on Main Street at the south end of town. The interurban ceased running after the new cement superhighway Illinois State Route 51 was opened in 1920 and automobiles became more prevalent, causing less business for the rail line.

One of the interurban cars can be seen on its track in front of Harry Richardson's home on the southwest corner of Main and Bridge Streets. The interurban ran each hour from 6:00 a.m. until midnight. The house was destroyed by fire in 1936, leaving a vacant lot for many years. Sometime later, a J&L gas station occupied the site, which has since become a vacant lot once again.

Three

Bricks and Pavement

James Thompson's three-story gristmill stood about a block east of his house, which still exists at 10639 Pearl Street. Brothers James and Asa Abbott were the gristmill operators and lived in a large house on the southwest corner of Bridge and Mulberry Streets. A cooper shop stood south of the mill on the Kinnikinnick Creek bank, where a Mr. Gardner made barrels for the Abbotts' flour. The two girls sitting in front of the old stone mill in this image are Mary Wilcox (left) and Ellen Roberts. The children peeking out of the mill are unidentified.

This is a view of James Thompson's 1840s gristmill and the race alongside Kinnikinnick Creek built for Thompson by Amos Tuttle, who also constructed many of the stone and brick homes in the village. An economic boom began in 1840 when Thompson arrived from Canada and started a woolen factory, gristmill, foundry for heavy-machine castings, and a distillery. The three-story gristmill was the first in the town.

This pre-1900 view is looking west from the top of the mill. The picture was taken by Mary Fyler, whose initials are scratched in the emulsion on the glass negatives in the lower right corner of the image. In the early days, when few owned cameras, people shared their pictures. Consequently, identical photographs can often be found in many different family albums.

46

Th.s footbridge across South Kinnikinnick Creek connected Pearl Street on the south with First Street on the north, providing a more convenient way for people living north of the creek to commute to work at James Thompson's mills. The woolen factory—the first one west of Detroit—was located south of South Kinnikinnick Creek and east of Pearl Street and began in 1847 with carding machines, dyeing vats, and spinning and weaving looms. This unidentified woman is testing the ice on the creek. In later years, it was possible to drive through the creek at this location near the bridge, and when cars became more common, people often drove into the water to clean their vehicles, making the site Roscoe's first "car wash."

Early settlers of Roscoe were greatly opposed to the drinking of alcohol. Shortly after James Thompson built a second Roscoe distillery, a meeting of citizens was held on January 8, 1847, and the following solution was adopted: "Resolved, as the sense of this establishment of the manufacture of ardent spirits as injurious and destructive to our most precious social, moral and religious interests." A later 1910 newspaper article refers to the distillery output as "the drink that exhilarates but to kill, that robs the poor of health and the rich of wealth." This distillery was located near the woolen mill; the second, which stood farther up the creek on Hamborg Road, was later converted into another grist mill and then into a house. The distillery pictured here was destroyed in 1898 after sitting in disrepair for many years.

Legend says that the bricks for this building, erected in 1845 on the southeast corner of Main and Bridge Streets, were brought from Chicago by oxcart, and that the structure was once a station on the Underground Railroad. It is known that the building was at one time a stagecoach stop and hotel and is now used as a private residence. Its plank floors still show marks indicating that it had once been divided into very small rooms. In the early days, it also housed several businesses, including a pharmacy on the second floor and, in 1860, the shoe and boot shop of E.H. Randall and the shoe-repair shop of David Sturtevant. In 1850, Dr. Giles Ransom was living here, and when he was appointed postmaster it became the site of the post office. (Courtesy of the *Rockford Register Star.*)

Alex McColl works in the Roscoe Creamery, built in 1894 by Harris Hardy, Joe Atwood, and Ed Randall. It was operated by Andrew Bender, who also kept the books and cleaned at the end of each work day, for the Rockford Union Dairy about 1913.

The creamery was located on the east side of Main Street at Elm Street, now the present site of the Roscoe Police Station. The Harnden home, to the right of the creamery, is still standing. The creamery closed around 1920 and burned in the early 1930s when being used by James Snook as a meat market.

Postmistress Mary Hinckley stands in front of the post office located on Main Street just north of the creek. She was postmistress from 1885 to 1890 and again from 1893 until her death in 1908—for a total of about 20 years. This picture was taken before the interurban tracks were put down in 1902.

On September 2, 1909, the Roscoe Post Office was located on the west side of Main Street just north of the Kinnikinnick Creek Bridge, which later became the site of the fire station. The interurban tracks, installed seven years earlier, can be seen in the center of Main Street. The building on the far right side, at the corner of Main and River Streets, is the early location of McRoberts's blacksmith shop.

Edward Baldwin, Roscoe's first rural mail carrier, is shown in his mail wagon out on delivery.

McRoberts's blacksmith shop stood at the southwest corner of Main and River Streets in earlier days. The sign in front advertises "Carriage & Wagon Repairing, Horseshoeing & Plow Work." That corner is currently the site of a log cabin built by Don Fry as a restaurant in the 1930s or 1940s.

W.W. Budd's blacksmith shop on Bridge Street had a versatile and booming business—except when it came to shoeing horses, which he left to the other blacksmiths in town.

William W. Budd works in his blacksmith shop, where he bought and sold buggies, wagons, and farm implements. He later sold ventilators or cupolas for barns and stanchions for cows. Budd worked on buggy and wagon tires, put new points on plows, sharpened cultivators, and repaired cutters and bobsleds.

This is Budd's blacksmith shop on Bridge Street as it looked in 1936. Dorothy Warner (on tricycle) and her cousin Beryl Sturtevant (in pedal car) are pictured with Oliver Goff, a family friend. The house in the background at the southwest corner of Bridge and Mulberry Streets was removed a few years ago, and a veterinarian's office now stands on the site. The blacksmith shop location is now a parking area for Sophia's Restaurant.

Arthur Briscoe's greenhouse, providing bouquets for all occasions, was located on the northeast corner of Mulberry and Grove Streets behind Budd's blacksmith shop during the early 1900s.

On March 13, 1903, G.H. Burt reopened his store at the northwest corner of Main and Bridge Streets. It had been newly papered and painted and featured a new hardwood floor, counter, and fixtures. Assisted by James Randall and George Stewart, Burt did a thriving business all day and evening. Customers were entertained by a gramophone and, while waiting to be served, the ladies were treated with candy and gum, and the gentlemen were given cigars. In the picture, Burt's wagon waits outside his store.

In the 1800s, O'Conner's hardware store sat on the west side of Main Street, just north of the Masonic and Woodmen Lodge buildings. The Harlem-Roscoe fire station is now located at the site. The Roscoe Improvement Association replaced the wooden boardwalks in the area with concrete sidewalks shortly after 1910.

Lorenzo Fyler works inside his store on Main Street. Fyler arrived in Roscoe in 1841 and ran a notion wagon. Later, he saw the need for a pharmacy and grocery store, so when his daughter, Mary, graduated from the Chicago Pharmacy College in 1889, she joined him in the renamed L.S. Fyler & Company.

These children walk along the boardwalk in front of Fyler's shop prior to 1900. The Harnden home and the creamery can be seen across Main Street on the left, with the pavilion and another house on the right.

Two storekeepers visit in front of Fyler's store on Main Street. After the 1926 fire, Harry Evans had his grocery store in the new building until 1945.

Lorenzo Fyler takes a break in front of his store on Main Street with his family's dog, Pedro. The creamery smokestack is visible at right, down the street, in the area now occupied by the police station and village hall.

Mary Fyler works in her father's store on Main Street. She joined her father after graduating from the Chicago Pharmacy College in 1889, the only girl in her class of 32.

Mary Fyler rides her bicycle northwest across Bridge Street toward Main Street and Burt's store in this early picture. Harry Richardson's house, seen to the left, was destroyed by fire in 1936. Note the wooden sidewalk and unpaved streets.

Near the turn of the century, Mary Fyler holds her bicycle and the paw of her family's dog, Pedro, outside her father's store on Main Street. Pedro is present in many of the pictures taken by Mary.

A young citizen smiles as she waits on the boardwalk in front of Lorenzo Fyler's store on Main Street. The raised platform made for easier boarding of buggies and wagons.

Pedro (left) and another dog wait while Lorenzo Fyler adjusts his hat in front of the stores at Main and Bridge Streets.

In the late 1880s, a man pulls up his wagon in front of the Main Street stores to purchase his supplies. General stores stocked nearly everything a family needed, including work clothes and boots, food, and tools. Going to town for supplies often meant an escape from chores and a time to meet friends and catch up on news.

David A. Sturtevant's store, located on the southeast corner of Main and Harrison Streets, also housed the post office during the 1930s, with Maude Sturtevant as postmistress. The Sturtevant home was directly behind the store, which was destroyed by fire in the mid-1930s.

Although the left part of this photograph is not good, the image still offers a view of the inside of D.A. Sturtevant's general store. The store was built by A.D. Lawrence in 1855 and was purchased by his clerk, David A. Sturtevant, when Lawrence moved away.

This Meat Market and Agriculture Warehouse was located along the east side of Main Street between Harrison and the creek bridge, and this image dates to before 1910, when the Roscoe Improvement Association began replacing the town's wooden walkways with cement sidewalks, many of which are still in use.

Here, a Main Street business is being improved upon with new construction.

The Ransom Manor stood on Main Street in the center of Roscoe, south of the creek. Built in 1869 by Amos Tuttle for physician Giles Ransom, it was partially destroyed by fire and was razed in 1989. It stood on the former site of the log cabin home of Dr. Solomon Jenks, Roscoe's first physician, and served as the home and office of numerous subsequent physicians.

SPECIAL CHICKEN DINNERS.   ROOMS FOR TOURISTS.
WE SPECIALIZE IN BANQUETS AND PARTIES.

This postcard shows the Ransom Manor during the time it served as a restaurant called Ye Olde English Tavern. When Dr. Jenks died in 1841, he was succeeded by Dr. Alfred Ames, Dr. Giles Ransom's teacher. Giles's two sons, Penn and Wilmot, also became physicians. Others who had offices in the building included Dr. Sikes, around 1900, and Dr. Walter Crocket, who practiced from 1896 until 1905. (Courtesy of the North Suburban Library.)

Known as the Masonic block on South Main Street, these buildings were destroyed by fire in 1926. At the left in this image, on the corner of Bridge and Main Streets, is the store and home of Art Ransom. Beside it is the Neblock home, then the Masonic hall, and the store and post office of Frank Moore was on the end. North of the Masonic building (out of view to the right) were the Modern Woodmen Lodge and O'Conner's hardware store. The last building held, at various times, an ice cream parlor or shoe shop. The 1902 interurban tracks are seen in the center of Main Street, along with the overhead electric wires.

After a fire on November 10, 1926, destroyed the original Masonic building, this facility was built at a cost of $35,000. The members did much of the work under the direction of architect and fellow member Harry Hardy. The cornerstone was laid on April 30, 1927. The Frank Wolf home is on the right.

Bert Shaw (left) and his brother Clare stand beside a load of watermelons in front of their home on Harrison Street, south of Leland Park.

One of Roscoe's most picturesque landmarks was this round barn on Atwood Road. Originally built and displayed at the 1893 World's Fair in Chicago, it was purchased, taken apart, and rebuilt in Roscoe, where it stood until 1977. It was then torn down to make way for a subdivision. As the photograph indicates, it proved to be a popular subject for artists.

The town hall at 5637 Broad Street was destroyed by fire in 1924 and was rebuilt, with the first meeting in the new structure being held on January 9, 1926. In addition to hosting township meetings, it also functioned as a community center. During the war, the Red Cross held first aid and knitting classes here. The building was sold to Hope Evangelical Free Church in 1971 and was later purchased by the Catholic Church of the Holy Spirit in 1979.

In this picture from April 9, 1907, the 1851 Methodist Episcopal church is visible at the corner of Main and Broad Streets. The last services in the building were held 10 days later, and the church was torn down later that month. Members had been afraid that the bell tower was in danger of falling; in attempting to pull it down, however, the workers were surprised to learn that this was not the case, and razing the building caused considerable difficulty.

In this similar view from April 17, 1932, which looks north on Main Street from the Sturtevant store at the southeast corner of Harrison and Main Streets, one can see the 1907 Methodist church in the next block. The two-story brick home at the left was built as a hotel by Samuel Lathrop out of bricks made in Roscoe at Coffin's brickyard. Most of these buildings are still standing.

For many years, this Shell station, built and operated by George McDonald in 1927, was Roscoe's only gas station. It was located at the northeast corner of Main and Bridge Streets. George and his wife, Pearl, lived behind the station with their two sets of twins—Verna and Virginia and Richard and Roger—in the two-story house that can be seen at the right edge of the picture. (Courtesy of Linda and Robert McAffee.)

Ralph Barnes (left) and George McDonald service a car at McDonald's Shell station. The station continued to sell gas into the 1980s, then operated as a repair shop until it was closed and torn down after the turn of the 21st century. (Courtesy of the McDonald family.)

Four

STEEPLES OF ROSCOE

The Methodist Episcopal church in Roscoe was organized in September 1836 when seven members met with an itinerant preacher named Samuel Pillsbury. They first met in homes before moving to a log blacksmith shop, which was also used as the school. When they could not afford to build, four settlers—Robert Cross, Benjamin Richardson, Henry Abell, and John Rhodes—constructed the stone basement with their own funds.

Roscoe's newly completed Methodist Episcopal church, on the northwest corner of Main and Broad Streets, was dedicated on June 15, 1851. Behind the church, on the left, is the first parsonage. Sheds for the horses, buggies, and wagons during bad weather were also behind the building.

The interior of the Methodist Episcopal church is pictured here during the dedication in 1851.

The brass bell for the Methodist church was cast in New York and brought to Roscoe in 1856 to be hung in the belfry. When the old church building was razed in 1907 for fear that the bell tower was unsafe, the bell was stored. It was later put in the belfry of the new church, where it is still rung most days at noon and calls the faithful to church on Sundays. (Courtesy of Roscoe United Methodist Church.)

This is a picture of an early funeral in the Methodist church. The deceased woman is unidentified. To the left, behind her picture, is the lectern, holding the large Bible used during services. The lectern, hand carved by Will Harley, is still displayed in the church.

Original members of the Methodist church pose for a 50th-anniversary photograph in front of the church in 1886. Pictured are, from left to right, (first row) William Cole, Asa Fitch, Mrs. A. Tuttle, and Alonzo D. Lawrence; (second row) Frank Richardson, Charles Richardson, James Gregory, Fred Warner, Mrs. William Richardson, Mahala Ransom, Margaret McAffee, Mrs. Perry Welch, Mary Jane Wood, Louise Lovejoy, and Mrs. Alonzo D. Lawrence.

Methodist church members gather in front of the new building on its dedication day, December 15, 1907. The final service in the original building before its razing was held April 19, 1907, and the new structure was built and dedicated just eight months later.

This 1950s photograph shows the small living room of the Methodist parsonage during the pastorate of Arthur Blaisdell. The parsonage was located directly behind the church. In the 1960s and 1970s, as membership grew, a new parsonage was built a few blocks away, and this structure was used for Sunday school classes.

The Roscoe Methodist Church is shown here as it looked in the 1960s. There have been several additions built to the church since it was constructed in 1907, but it is still located in the same place as the original building, with two additional entrances of the same Dutch-bonnet design.

In the first Methodist church building, the choir sang from a balcony at the back of the church. In the new, 1907 building, the choir sang from the front of the sanctuary, as shown in this picture from dedication day, December 15, 1907.

These ladies performed a pantomime for the Women's Home Missionary Society meeting at the Methodist church in 1925. Jennie Richardson, standing second from the right, sang. Lenore Sturtevant holds a banjo; the others are unidentified.

Rev. Ray Baldwin and his wife, Marjory, stand before the Roscoe Methodist Church during the two-day 125th-anniversary celebration on October 14 and 15, 1961.

The First Community Congregational Church was chartered in 1844 with 18 members. Meetings were held on the top floor of the seminary building until the church was built at the southeast corner of Broad and Third Streets on a site donated by Alvan and Solomon Leland.

This is an early view of the still-unpaved Broad Street looking west toward the Congregational church. The church still looks much the same. In the distance on the right, the belfry of the Roscoe Grade and High School can be seen. In the distance straight down Broad Street, the bell tower of the Methodist Episcopal church is visible. (Courtesy of the North Suburban Library.)

The interior of the Congregational church, erected in 1854, is shown here in the early 1900s. Until it was completed, members met in the upper story of Alvan Leland's seminary on Harrison Street. Leland had been elected deacon of the church at its formational meetings in 1843.

On Children's Day in June 1898, the interior of the Congregational church is decorated with the United States flag.

Dr. Samuel W. Eaton and his wife are shown here in their home. He was a beloved pastor who served the Congregational church for 15 years around the turn of the century. Their son was Dr. E.D. Eaton, president of Beloit College.

Five

LEARNIN' AND TIME TOGETHER

Wooden planks form a walkway up what some called "the hill of knowledge," where the Roscoe School was built in 1855. The first floor held the primary and intermediate rooms, while the high school was located on the upper floor.

This undated postcard shows Roscoe students on the front steps of the two-story, four-room, redbrick school on Main Street, which was built by Amos Tuttle in 1855.

In this early photograph of Roscoe Grade School, built on a hill, the schoolyard is full of children. The large playground in front of the building was filled with students on sleds during recess in the winter.

The invitation to the 1909 Roscoe High School graduation (held at the Methodist Episcopal church on June 15) had an outer parchment cover with a purple ribbon threaded through to show the class colors of purple and white. Inside, the program and the names of the 11 graduates are printed.

On August 8, 1899, these former Roscoe High School students gathered around the organ and wrote their names on the blackboard for their picture. They are, in unknown order, Mabel Wood, Julia McAffee Worcester, Blanche Sturtevant Baldwin, Minnie L. Richardson, Mary Rhodes Wilcox, Maude Sturtevant, Cora Baldwin, and Ellen Roberts.

This group met for its annual reunion in 1900. Reunions were held for over 20 years and featured a program with former students performing for their peers with skits, plays, and poetry readings.

WINNEBAGO COUNTY, ILLINOIS

Eighth Grade Examination, May 4, 1918

Afternoon.

CIVICS.

Answer six questions.

1. Name two ways in which Congress may borrow money.

2. What is meant by Civil Service?

3. Give an example of an ex post facto law.

4. What is meant by Liberty Loan? Thrift Stamps?

5. Who is governor of Illinois? When was he elected, and how long is his term?

6. How was the right to vote given to the negroes?

7. (a) How does the selective draft differ from the draft during the Civil War?

   (b) In what way might a man evade his war service during the Civil War?

   (c) Is it possible for him to evade the selective draft by the same method?

8. What is the Thirteenth amendment?

9. How may the Constitution be amended?

10. What proposed amendment is engaging the attention of the people at present?

In 1918, all eighth graders in Winnebago County were required to pass a series of tests before graduating. The civics test required students to answer six of ten questions. The other tests included US history, grammar, geography, agriculture, and arithmetic.

82

This picture shows a classroom of older students at Roscoe Grade School in 1921. Note the old organ at the left and the clock on the rear wall. Some of the pictures on the wall were still being used in the 1930s.

Principal P.W. Peterson sits at his desk in the Roscoe Grade School around 1900.

This is a picture of Roscoe Grade School on a postcard that was mailed July 30, 1930. By that time, Hononegah High School had been open for 10 years, and Roscoe's high school students no longer attended here.

Around 1900, the pupils of teacher P.W. Peterson gave him a surprise party. In the early days, there were two adults per classroom: a woman to teach and a man to keep order.

84

In April 1944, a tornado took off part of the roof of the Roscoe Grade School shortly before classes were to start. Primary students finished out the school year in the town hall. Fifth and sixth grades met in the Methodist church, and seventh and eighth graders attended their classes in the Masonic hall. That summer, the school's second story was removed and the two rooms on the lower level were cut in half, making four rooms to hold eight grades. Classes continued in these cramped rooms until the new Kinnikinnick Consolidated School District opened in 1949.

Students at Burr Oak School sit in front of the school in their costumes for the 1925–1926 graduation play. Their teacher that year was Lenore Sturtevant. Burr Oak School was organized in the 1850s and closed in 1948.

Students at Roscoe Grade School in the 1930s pose on the school's front steps. They are, from left to right, (first row) Gene Bolander, Beryl Sturtevant, Lois Wood, Dorothy Warner, Anita Bell Brown, and Marcus Adwell; (second row) Roy Muchmore, Clarence Barber, and unidentified.

Students Earl (left), Milton (center), and Wayne wait with their sleds outside Shaw School for a little sledding at recess. Shaw School began around 1856 at the northwest corner of Elevator and Love Roads. It was closed in 1942, with the one remaining student being sent to attend Roscoe School.

HO-NO-NE-GAH COMMUNITY HIGH SCHOOL
1921

This photograph shows the new Hononegah Community High School's student body, faculty and school board in front of the entrance to the new building on the edge of Rockton. Eight seniors, ten juniors, nine sophomores, and twenty-six freshmen were enrolled that first year according to the inaugural school annual, which the following year would be named the *Mack* in honor of the school namesake's husband, early settler Stephen Mack.

HO-NO-NE-GAH FOOTBALL SQUAD
1921

In January 1920, the formation of a community high school district was explored. Territories were studied, and the district was formed consisting of Roscoe and Rockton townships, with the new school opening in the fall of 1920 and named for the Winnebago Indian princess Ho-No-Ne-Gah, who married Stephen Mack, the area's first white settler. The first football team was formed the following fall, with only one of the team members ever before having played the sport.

Kinnikinnick Consolidated School, built on Pine Lane—a block west of the old 1855 building—opened in 1949 with 231 students and John Mohring as principal. Roscoe, Burr Oak, Shaw, Windy Peak, and McColl schools consolidated to form the new district. By 1961, the nine-room building had expanded to 19 classrooms and administrative offices, with 475 students under the leadership of superintendent and principal Wallace Hanson. The area continued to grow, and Ledgewood School opened in 1975 with Robert Lauber as principal. Stone Creek School opened in 1990, and Roscoe Middle School in 2000. The four schools together now constitute the Kinnikinnick Consolidated School District 131.

Six

FUN AND GAMES

Roscoe's Brass Band was famous in the town's early days and played for the laying of the cornerstone at Beloit College on June 24, 1847. Neither Beloit nor Rockford had an orchestra at that time, and Roscoe was the musical center of the area. Members of the band are, from left to right, (seated) unidentified; Henry Curtis, tuba player; unidentified; Rubie Curtis, on cornet; Ernest Wilson; Giles Baldwin, who played trombone; and unidentified; (standing) unidentified, Charles Rhodes, and Art Ransom.

In *Nature's Byways* is an operetta written by Florence Lovejoy when she was 12. It was performed at the Methodist church on May 29, 1921, and later published. The cast includes Mary Parker as Sunshine, Inez Richardson as Spring, Annie Burch as Birds, Louisa Wilcox as Rain, Genivieve Cummings as King Winter, Hazel Hendershott as Ice, and Florence Belden as Snow. (Courtesy of the North Suburban Library.)

A group of women holds a quilting bee at Fyler's in 1898. Women often helped each other make quilts, and church groups often made quilts for raffles and other occasions.

In this photograph from May 15, 1899, Giles Baldwin plays a trombone in his apartment above Sturtevant's store. A violin and mandolin wait on the table, a guitar rests against the table, and a valve trombone leans against his chair.

Mr. and Mrs. Fred Warner Jr. spend time reading outside in the 1800s.

At a musicale held at the Bradley home, Will Bradley plays the violin and Kate Bradley, the piano. Standing behind them are, from left to right, Mary Fyler, Rubie Curtis, Alice Curtis, Henry Curtis, Carrie Bradley, unidentified, and Gertrude Smith. In 1906, Will Bradley had a song called "When the Parlor Lamp Goes Down" published by the Thompson Music Company of Chicago.

Two unidentified girls read their mail beside the Rock River sometime around 1900.

Six people lie on their stomachs on the grass. This photograph is captioned, "on the grass to bleach," which refers to the practice in those days of putting white things on the grass to dry (and whiten) after being washed.

From the smiles on their faces, this group seems to be having a good time. The album caption labels this "a frolic at Aunt Sarah's."

Seen here is an 1800s kitchen with the kettle on the stove and a man working at the table. The caption calls him "a new 'hand' in the kitchen."

In the 1800s, young people ice-skate on the frozen creek east of the old steel Main Street Bridge in the center of town. The creek was a popular spot for ice-skating in the winter and for swimming in the summer.

This group met around the turn of the century to play croquet. The lady seated on the ground is unidentified. The others are, from left to right, (first row) Charles and Belle Richardson and Mrs. William Richardson; (second row) Mrs. Knope, Alice Curtis, B.F. Richardson III, Sue Whitlock, Chicago resident James Gaffney, Fred Nichols, Sophia Atwood, Henry Curtis, Priscilla Nichols, Rubie Lovejoy, Wyman Lovejoy, Mate Beaman, and Margaret and Lionel Richardson.

Members of a young family learn to ride their bicycles in the early 1900s. According to the album caption, they are "ready for a race." Bicycle riding was a favorite activity of those lucky enough to own a bicycle. Children in town rode bikes to and from school and often spent their free time riding with friends up and down the streets of Roscoe.

A group of children holds a parade at the intersection of Broad and Main Streets in July 1898. The picture is captioned, "How we will make the Spanish run." The redbrick house behind them, a former stagecoach stop, is still standing.

In this late-1800s photograph, two unidentified women fish in the creek near the old mill.

This trio of children must have been in some sort of contest or performance. The caption on the photograph reads, "Wigwam, Winner, August 8, 1901"

In 1936, four young neighborhood children have a parade on the sidewalk along Bridge Street. Leading the parade with a drum is Dorothy Warner, followed by Bobby Dobson in the pedal car and Virgil Silbaugh providing music. Beryl Sturtevant brings up the rear on roller skates.

A group of people seems to be on a fun outing with buggies. Note the parasols carried by the women. Before automobiles arrived on the scene, the horse and buggy was used for sightseeing and outings with friends, as well as for transportation.

A buggy load of people waits patiently at the corner of Main and Harrison Streets around 1900. The 1850 Methodist Episcopal church can be seen in the background.

In June 1898, friends have gathered for a party at the Fyler home to say goodbye to Grace Colton, who was leaving for the West.

Preparing a barbecue at Camp Frolic on June 2, 1900, are, from left to right, Henry Curtis, Frank Cummings, Cliff Wilcox, and Giles Baldwin. The people of Roscoe had many barbecues at local picnic spots to mark special occasions.

This picture was taken August 1, 1891, at Camp Fairplay, which was held that year at Lyford's Grove across the river. Camp Fairplay was held in various places in the summer for the young men and women of Roscoe. They put up tents, played tennis and other games, swam, and rode in canoes and boats. In the evening, parents brought the evening meal, and everyone ate together. Up and down the river and the creek were privately owned areas of land where citizens were allowed to picnic and play. Leland Park, formerly called Roosevelt Park, was the only public park at the time. Over the years, four more parks have been added to accommodate the sports and leisure interests of Roscoe residents.

This picnic was held on the lawn at the home of Andrew James Lovejoy on August 5, 1898.

In 1898, eating out had a different meaning than it does today. Here, a group eats dinner outside on the lawn on August 8, 1898. With no air-conditioning, the weather in August was often very warm and humid, and people looked forward to dining outside to enjoy the breeze and escape their hot kitchens. Many had no outside furniture and carried their tables and chairs outside for dinner.

In this c. 1900 photograph, the family gathers at the Lundy residence for Thanksgiving.

Marguerite Hardy takes a break and catches a drink of water from her neighbor's pump at 5440 Bridge Street in 1925. The well and pump were shared by the homes on each side, rather than each family having their own.

This woman and young boy are beside themselves in the garden thanks to trick photography.

Some fancy photography techniques of the time make it appear that this gentleman is having a conversation with himself.

Maude Sturtevant is the focus of trick photography in the early 1900s. The eldest of three daughters born to David and Harriet Sturtevant, she was a teacher for many years, as well as tax collector and postmistress. She died in 1922.

Giles Baldwin appears to be a set of quadruplets in this early-1900s photographic experiment.

Blanche and Giles Baldwin play the guitar and mandolin in their apartment around 1900. Other instruments rest in the corner. At the time, Roscoe's 20th Century Club was flourishing, and members met to study and learn about culture, classics, literature, and world events. Each monthly meeting was devoted to a different topic, and members were often entertained by music, readings, or skits. It is possible that the Baldwins were preparing for one of these performances. Another club custom was to answer the roll call with a quotation from the writer being studied. The club was active for over 20 years.

Seven

FACES OF ROSCOE

In this 1800s image, Belle Knowlton stands in the front (west) yard of the Curtis home, located on the east side of Main Street at the corner of Broad Street. Knowlton was the daughter of Sabin and Mary Jane Wood. Sabin was a choir director of the Methodist church. It was said he had a great tenor voice and could have been a professional singer. He had singing schools in Roscoe, Beloit, and Caledonia.

David A. Sturtevant poses in the early 1900s in front of his store at the southeast corner of Main and Harrison Streets. With him is a young Florence Lovejoy (Shugars), who lived in the house seen behind them at the northeast corner of the block.

Looking east on Harrison Street from Main, one can see a home where Dr. Alfred Ames (Roscoe's second physician) lived in 1844, and where Dr. Edward Sikes resided around the turn of the century. Dr. Ames organized the first two Masonic lodges in Winnebago County in Roscoe and Rockton before moving to Minnesota, where he started a Masonic organization in Minneapolis.

James W. Smith rests inside his home. In 1862, he and his brother George were two of twenty Roscoe high school boys who volunteered to fight for the Union when his principal, James B. Kerr, who had recently become county superintendent of schools, resigned to raise a company of volunteers. Kerr was later killed during battle. George returned from the war in 1865 and went to Cross Grove; cut two smooth, straight poles; spliced them together; and fastened them to the front of the school. This became the first flagstaff raised over a district school in the United States in memory of the boys and teacher who had given their lives in defense of the flag.

Frank and Nettie Cummings and Henry and Alice Curtis visit with unidentified friends. No one is specifically identified. In the early days, with no television or radio, a visit with friends was an enjoyable way to spend time. When people went to the home of a friend for dinner, even if they lived close, it was often printed in the newspaper as reported by the local correspondent.

Several families in Roscoe were named Hardy, and this image shows the H.W. Hardy family. In 1855, after the new school was built, the Methodist church basement was no longer being used for classes. Hosea Hardy, who had been hired as church janitor and could not find housing, moved his family into the vacated area. His daughter Belle was born while they lived there and was named in honor of her birthplace.

Hazel and Gus Wood (seated) and an unidentified woman enjoy a moment's rest outside on the lawn. Gus was the youngest of 13 children. He and his family came to Roscoe from Maine in 1850, when he was 10. Hazel was one of his two daughters. He was first married to Martha McAffee and later married Hattie Cleave. He fought in the Civil War and was a Seventh-day Adventist.

Perry Welch had a wagon-making and -repair business on the west side of Main Street, south of River Street, in the old seminary building he had moved from the northeast corner of Harrison and Second Streets. The upper room was a meeting hall for the Good Templars, and the lower room housed his shop. The building eventually burned. Welch became known for killing Roscoe's last black bear in 1842.

Dr. W.H. Shaw waits in his buggy in front of Fyler's store. Roscoe was blessed with many good physicians and veterinarians during the early years. In 1839, Dr. Lent B. Bradley arrived in town, the first dentist west of Chicago. His home and office were on Bridge Street, now the southeast corner of Bridge Street and Illinois State Highway 251.

This group of friends met in the early 1900s to enjoy activities and outings. They are, from left to right, Ellen Roberts, Clara Bradley, unidentified, Priscilla Nichols, unidentified, Charles Rhodes, Marie Rhodes, H.V. Holt, Alvin Wilcox, May Wilcox, Wyman Lovejoy, and Minnie Richardson. (Courtesy of Robert Lawhorn.)

L.W. Richardson holds his grandchild in his home for a picture around 1900. Richardson came to Roscoe in 1854. A blacksmith, he invented and patented the Roscoe Diamond riding plow, guaranteed to "scour wet or dry." At 4:00 a.m. on June 3, 1858, Richardson rescued Reverend Ilsley from Roscoe's great flood.

On her way to do some shopping at Fyler's store in the late 1800s, Susanna Palmer walks along the boardwalk with her market basket. Palmer lived across the street from the Methodist parsonage, which was located behind the Methodist church.

Kay McCurry, seen here, was the husband of Alice McCurry, who wrote the many Fall Festival pageants. Kay was active in the organization of Hononegah High School and served as the president of the first board of education. He also filled the position of Roscoe Township supervisor from 1920 to 1941. (Courtesy of Robert Lawhorn.)

This is the first board of education of Hononegah Community High School, which began in the fall of 1920. Kay McCurry is in the center (with the mustache). On the far right is F.F. Moore, also of Roscoe. The other members of the board—unidentified in this image—are secretary C.E. Phelps, W.W. Liddle, and E.B. Manley. (Courtesy of the *Rockford Register Star* and Robert Lawhorn.)

Alice Dodge McCurry, wife of Kay McCurry, wrote the well-known Roscoe Fall Festival pageants. Her way of securing participation was to assign certain segments to different area groups or organizations, give them an outline, and allow the participants to use their own ideas and creativity. An accomplished artist, McCurry also designed and painted most of the backdrops for the presentations.

The Women's Christian Temperance Union (WCTU) holds a meeting at Emily Lundy's home around 1900. The people of Roscoe were much opposed to drinking, and this group and others were very active in their efforts to curb the practice. There were no public taverns or bars in the early years, and only one—the still-operating Whiffletree—operated throughout much of the 20th century.

Fred Warner tests the water from one of his wells. Warner, his mother, and three sisters came in 1837 via the Great Lakes to join his father, Walter, in Roscoe. The voyage took three weeks.

Dr. Will Baldwin, veterinarian, sets out from his home on Broad Street to make his rounds on October 17, 1903.

Amos and Allie Sammons sit in front of their home on Bridge Street. Allie was an organist and pianist. The home, which has since been enlarged and renovated, currently operates as a portion of Sophia's Restaurant.

Pictured here in 1909, the Taft home still sits today across Broad Street from Leland Park. The photograph was taken from the front of the Congregational church parsonage.

Bruno the dog gets a ride in Dr. W.H. Shaw's carriage with an unidentified woman and Grace Colton (right).

Gus Wood (left) and George Wiggins cut firewood behind the home of Hattie Sturtevant at 5440 Bridge Street around the turn of the century. Wiggins, a tailor in Belvidere, later married Hattie, daughter of David A. Sturtevant.

Dale Sturtevant shows off his catch in front of his boyhood home in the 1930s. The son of Frank and Bertha Sturtevant, Dale lived at 5466 Bridge Street with his wife, Gladys, and children, Beryl and Phyllis, before moving to Minnesota and then to Phoenix, Arizona, where he worked at Motorola as a machinist and inventor. Fishing was easy with the Rock River just down at the end of the street.

An unidentified man stands in the street with his workhorse, probably before 1900. The sides of businesses were frequently used for advertising. Here, groceries and coffee are advertised, and the edges of posters are also seen. In street scenes, posters are often seen tacked to every utility pole, and fences are frequently painted with advertisements for brands of household staples and businesses in nearby towns.

Rev. Quincy Dowd and his dog Roscoe visit with George Miller at his mail wagon as it stops in front of the Congregational church parsonage across from Leland Park. (Courtesy of the North Suburban Library.)

These folks say goodbye to Grace Colton (right) as she departs for Nebraska. Her trunks are seen tied into the wagon for the trip to the station. At the time, many area people were moving to Nebraska or other western states as part of the great westward expansion.

This picture, taken in August 1898, is captioned, "Our Jessie." Jessie is petting Pedro, Mary Fyler's dog, at Fyler's house on Bridge Street. Many of the pictures in the old albums were taken by Mary at her home when friends and relatives visited.

Joe S. Scholten, a horseshoer from Roscoe, stands beside his mobile business with the tools of his trade displayed before him. Scholten made and prepared most of his shoes in his Roscoe smithy, then traveled throughout southern Wisconsin and northern Illinois plying his trade. He began to learn his occupation at the age of 14, serving an apprenticeship of four years, and later spent many years working on race-, track, saddle, and show horses, shoeing an average of 70 animals a week.

P.A. Peterson, teacher, says goodbye to his wife at the gate as he leaves for school with a load of books. Throughout the years, Roscoe has been blessed with excellent teachers and schools, with an emphasis on education. Many of the settlers arriving from the East had excellent educations and wanted the same for their children.

Reverend Cormack poses with his wife and son Joseph in the Methodist parsonage during his 1897–1900 pastorate. The parsonage was built by the parishioners behind the church at 5432 Broad Street between 1857 and 1858, under the direction of Rev. Lewis Anderson, who had been a carpenter before becoming a minister.

Henry Rhodes sits in his living room as his picture is taken. Both Henry and his brother J.M. Rhodes enlisted in the Civil War with school principal Kerr in 1862. In 1840, their father, John Rhodes, had built Roscoe's second sawmill at the mouth of Kinnikinnick Creek.

Mary Armsby sits at the foot of a wooden glider swing with her family, enjoying a glass of lemonade at the Armsby home, called Riverside. On the right are the ladder and framework of their windmill. The Armsbys owned a broom factory on Main Street.

Members of the Women's Society of Christian Service are pictured with their children in front of the Methodist church in October 1956. The members, from left to right, are (front row) Ruth Bumstead, Ruth Mock, Lois Mutimer, and Dorothy Denbow; (back row) Bertha Hardy, Maxine Cummings, Barbara Harshbarger, Ethel O'Dell, A. Turner, E. Whiting, Nina Ahlquist, unidentified, Hattie Rogers, Flossie Oakes, Nellie Cummings, Lenore Warner, S. Peters, and Minnie Hayes. The children are not identified.

Charles Richardson, father of Ellen (left), Lillie (center), and Minnie, arrived in Roscoe, on October 17, 1836, with his parents and 10-month-old sister, Abigail, after a four-month journey from Michigan. Richardson's parents, Benjamin Richardson II and Mary Ann, were two of the seven settlers who met to organize the Methodist church shortly after arrival.

This is a picture of J.M. Rhodes with his granddaughters. Rhodes, born in 1840, was one of the high school boys who volunteered to join the Union army with school principal James Kerr in 1862. His father, John J. Rhodes, was elected Winnebago County supervisor in 1850.

The McAffee family enjoys a picnic. The McAffees are descendants of Roscoe's first settler, Robert J. Cross. Some of Cross's descendants still live in Roscoe today.

In the late 1800s and early 1900s, Dr. Will Baldwin, a local veterinarian, put many miles on his buggy calling on his patients at farms around Roscoe. The Baldwin family included five brothers who, through their lives and work, contributed to the history of Roscoe, as shown by the many images of them and their families.

Boys play with their bicycles and animals about a block west of Leland Park. The Congregational church steeple is visible in the background.

This is the first home of David A. Sturtevant. When it was destroyed by fire in 1904, the people of the village rallied around him and helped to build a new home on the site.

David A. Sturtevant's newly built home, located behind his store, is pictured here in 1905. This structure is still standing at 5541 Harrison Street.

Lizzie McCabe watches as Mary Fyler works in her garden. Lizzie's father was an Irish immigrant, and her parents came west by train from New Jersey shortly after being married in 1854. They then walked to Roscoe from Sterling, Illinois, carrying their trunk between them, and arrived in June 1855. In 1857, the McCabes' house was one of several destroyed by the flood. Lizzie was born in 1861, one of four children. She earned between $10 and $15 per month as a teacher. Later, she lived in Beloit and became a dressmaker for the wealthy. She died in 1957 at the age of 93.

Dr. and Mrs. Sikes and their daughter Marian are set for a drive. Marian Sikes was one of four babies born to a group of good friends in 1909. The others were Connie McCurry, Marian Hopkins, and Florence Lovejoy. The girls celebrated their birthdays together and remained close friends for many years.

Chauncey Jerome was the great-uncle of Winston Churchill. He came west and married Ann Wood, and the couple lived at 5913 Chestnut Street (which has been recently remodeled). Jerome fought in the Civil War with the 8th Wisconsin Cavalry and is buried in an unmarked grave in the Roscoe cemetery.

Visit us at
arcadiapublishing.com

.

www.ingramcontent.com/pod-product-compliance
Lightning Source LLC
Chambersburg PA
CBHW050547110426
42813CB00008B/2278